Member of the
Evangelical Christian
Publishers Association

Printed in China.

You Are in My Prayers

ELLYN SANNA

Every day I offer
prayers of thanks for you.
I am rich for having known you,
and now I wish. . .and pray. . .
that you will enjoy those same riches in your own life.
I can't express with words all that I hope for you,
but I am asking God to surround you,
comfort you, and strengthen you
with His love and mercy,
even through days that are dark,
so that you will know
the peace of His will
working in your life.

Contents

The wings of prayer can carry high and far.

ANONYMOUS

Prayer is not
conquering God's reluctance,
but taking hold of God's willingness.

PHILLIPS BROOKS

More things are wrought by prayer
than this world dreams of.

ALFRED, LORD TENNYSON

1

Wishes. . .
and Prayers

*P*rayer, in its simplest definition,
is merely a wish turned God-ward.

PHILLIPS BROOKS

Every wish
is like a prayer—
with God.

ELIZABETH BARRETT BROWNING

I wish that you would feel encouraged. . .
and so I offer up this prayer:

Lord, please touch this one in her time of discouragement.
Give her patience to see the familiar in a new way.
With the new insight, give her strength to move forward.
I know You are able to communicate in unique ways.
Speak today.
You have resources beyond our comprehension.
Reveal them now.
You are the God of hope. Hope is needed now.
Hear my prayer, O Lord. Amen.

VIOLA RUELKE GOMMER

Prayer is the song of the heart.
It reaches the ear of God. . . .

KAHIL GIBRAN

Prayer is the little implement
Through which men reach
Where presence is denied them.

EMILY DICKINSON

Everywhere you trip is where a treasure lies.

NORMAN LEAR

Oh, how I wish good things for you!
You have meant so much to me,
done so much for me,
and blessed me so many times. . . .
I long for God to shower you with blessings in return.
So even when life trips you up,
when it seems like difficulties clutter your life
and impede your way,
I'm praying that beneath each and every obstacle
you'll find buried treasure,
planted there by God.

Today, if you feel discouraged,
or anxious,
or lonely,
please know that I am here,
united with you in prayer.
I wish you an abundance of
joy, love, peace, comfort, security,
and the knowledge of God's presence.

*Let's travel the path of prayer together.
We will find that shared burdens are
divided and easier to carry.
We will also find that our joys are doubled.
Everything is blessed when it is shared.*

VIOLA RUELKE GOMMER

To pray. . .is to desire, but it is to desire
what God would have us desire.
He who desires not from the bottom of his heart,
offers a deceitful prayer.

FÉNELON

Prayer is a cry of hope.

FRENCH PROVERB

Certain thoughts are prayers.
There are moments when,
whatever be the attitude of the body,
the soul is on its knees.

VICTOR HUGO

Prayer is love raised to its greatest power;
and the prayer of intercession is the noblest
and most Christian kind of prayer
because in it love—and imagination—
reach their highest and widest range.

ROBERT J. MCCRACKEN

"*But* if you stay joined to me
and my words remain in you,
you may ask any request you like,
and it will be granted!"

JOHN 15:7 NLT

*The deepest wishes of the heart
find expression in secret prayer.*

GEORGE E. REES

Your God has told you to open your mouth;
He has told you to open it wide,
and He has promised, "I will fill it. . . ."
You've been granted a license to yearn,
you have permission to be hungry—
so don't be afraid to
desire great mercies from the God of heaven.

JOHN BUNYAN

I'm longing for
God's blessings in your life.
I'm praying for His great mercies
to fill your heart.

The earnest prayer of a righteous person
has great power and wonderful results.

JAMES 5:16 NLT

2

Beyond Words

Sometimes I don't know what I should pray for you.
I don't know what you need most;
I don't know the answers to your life's dilemmas.
All I can do is come to God
and pour out my concern for you.
Without words, I put you in God's hands,
knowing that His love will always do
what's best.

When you pray,
better to have your heart be without words
than your words without heart. . . .
The best prayers have often more groans than words.

JOHN BUNYAN

Prayer requires more of the heart
than of the tongue.

ADAM CLARKE

While people are praying, God is searching their hearts to see what the Spirit is saying in the midst of all the human words. The Spirit speaks through their words, sighs, or groans, because it is only through Him that our prayers can be made according to the will of God.

JOHN BUNYAN

For we don't even know
what we should pray for,
nor how we should pray.
But the Holy Spirit prays for us
with groanings that cannot be
expressed in words.

ROMANS 8:26–27 NLT

I'm glad that God knows my heart.
He knows how much
I care about you.
His Spirit moves through my concern,
and turns it into prayer.

It is not your words that God looks at. It's not as
though He will only listen to you if you come to Him
with some eloquent speech. . . . You may not be able to
talk because there is too much trouble in your heart. . . .
When you are too anguished to speak, the Holy Spirit
stirs inside your heart with vehement groans and sighs.

JOHN BUNYAN

There can be prayers without words
just as well as songs, I suppose.

GEORGE BUSSON DUMAURIER

The simple heart that
freely asking in love,
obtains.

JOHN GREENLEAF WHITTIER

3

When Days Are Dark

The people walking in darkness
have seen a great light;
on those living in the land of the shadow of death
a light has dawned.

ISAIAH 9:2 NIV

When your days are dark,
I pray that you will see
the light of Christ,
shining even in the deepest shadows.

A Prayer for Dark Days

Lord, my heart is filled with darkness.
Where are You? I wait to hear Your voice of comfort.
I wait for You to bring light into my life now.
Where are You?
I long to have the darkness taken from my heart.
My lips are dry with longing.
I long for Your cup of refreshment.
Where are You?
I need Your comfort, hope, and living water.
I wait, alone and scared, in the dark.
I wait. . .and then I remember:
You will never leave me.
You are present, here, now, in the dark.
I am not alone.
I will wrap myself in the promise of Your presence.
Thank You, Lord.
Amen.

VIOLA RUELKE GOMMER

I have been driven many times to my knees
by the overwhelming conviction that
I had nowhere else to go.

ABRAHAM LINCOLN

Prayer is a force
as real as terrestrial gravity.
It supplies us with a flow of
sustaining power in our daily lives.

ALEXIS CARREL

Because of the LORD's great love

we are not consumed,

for his compassions never fail.

They are new every morning;

great is your faithfulness.

LAMENTATIONS 3:22–23 NIV

Today, may you sense the Lord's great love,
His unfailing compassion,
and His endless faithfulness.
No matter how overwhelming
the circumstances you face,
God will not allow them to swallow you up.
His love for you is always new.

Sometimes life seems like more than you can bear.
The days are filled with fear and uncertainty.
Look to God for hope.
He will give you:

Healing,
Opportunity,
Patience, and
Eagles' wings.

Look to God and God alone.
His strength will help you fly
up through the clouds into His light.

VIOLA RUELKE GOMMER

You Are in My Prayers

He gives strength to the weary
and increases the power of the weak. . . .
Those who hope in the LORD will renew their strength.
They will soar on wings like eagles;
they will run and not grow weary,
they will walk and not be faint.

ISAIAH 40:29, 31 NIV

*Rejoice in hope,
be patient in suffering,
persevere in prayer.*

ROMANS 12:12 NRSV

I'm persevering in prayer for you!
May the difficulties in your life give birth to endurance,
patience, new energy, and most of all. . .hope!

Some people think they are only in God's presence, renewed by His grace, when they feel comforted and cheery. Unfortunately, they never realize that God may be richly with them when they are in the depths of despair, when they cry out, "I am overwhelmed with depression," or "I am afraid and full of doubt."

. . .God's grace [has]. . .been coming to you all along, working in your heart in all these secret ways. . . .

JOHN BUNYAN

You can be sure that the more we undergo sufferings for Christ, the more he will shower us with his comfort and encouragement.

2 CORINTHIANS 1:5 TLB

"LORD, help!"
they cried in their trouble,
and he saved them from their distress.
He spoke, and they were healed—
snatched from the door of death.

PSALM 107:19–20 NLT

Jesus stood up and
commanded the wind, "Be quiet!"
and he said to the waves, "Be still!"
The wind died down,
and there was a great calm.

MARK 4:39 TEV

During the storms in your life, I pray that
you will call on Jesus to quiet the wind and the waves.
No matter how tossed about you are,
His voice will always bring great calm.

4

God's
Will

He is always moving about His work
to shape and arrange events
in His wise government of our lives.

JOHN OF THE CROSS

The steps of the godly are directed by the LORD.
He delights in every detail of their lives.

PSALM 37:23 NLT

Jehovah himself is caring for you! He. . .preserves your life.

PSALM 121:5, 7 TLB

Today,
and every day,
I pray that you will know
that God is caring for you
the way a careful mother watches over her child,
making sure the child is always safe.
Nothing can truly threaten you,
for you are wrapped in God's love.
He wants you to be full of joy.
May His will give you comfort and peace.

Life can be so confusing some days.
The way ahead is dark, full of twists and turns,
and forks in the road
where you don't know which way to go.
I'm praying God will make His will clear
to you and give you peace.

Whether you turn to the right
or to the left,

your ears will hear

a voice behind you,

saying, "This is the way; walk in it."

Isaiah 30:21 NIV

36

God's will for you is
wholeness,
health,
strength,
and never-ending joy.
I'm praying that you'll see God bring all these
to fulfillment
in your life.

For I will restore health to you,

and your wounds I will heal.

JEREMIAH 30:17 RSV

If you pray for something and don't receive it,
God may know you don't really need it.
He has promised to supply all your needs.
Delays in God's answer to your prayer may not be a
denial, though.
This may not be the perfect time,
and His timing is always perfect.

Now is the time to trust.

WINFIELD FRANK RUELKE

I pray that God will give you
wisdom in your asking,
patience in your waiting,
and a willing spirit to accept His answer.

God grant me the serenity to
accept the things I cannot change,
courage to change the things I can,
and the wisdom to know the difference.

REINHOLD NIEBUHR

The Lord is all I have, and so in him I put my hope.
The Lord is good to everyone who trusts in him,
So it is best for us to wait in patience—
to wait for him to save us.

LAMENTATIONS 3:24–26 TEV

Rely on God.

Wait.

Hope.

Be patient.

And know that you are always

in my prayers.